The Biography of Tomatoes

Adrianna Morganelli

 Crabtree Publishing Company
www.crabtreebooks.com

Crabtree Publishing Company

www.crabtreebooks.com

For my grandparents, Tony and Maria Morganelli

Coordinating editor: Ellen Rodger
Series editor: Carrie Gleason
Editor: L. Michelle Nielsen
Design and production coordinator: Rosie Gowsell
Production assistance and layout: Samara Parent
Art direction: Rob MacGregor
Photo research: Allison Napier
Prepress technician: Nancy Johnson

Photo Credits: Arco Images/Alamy: p. 20; Christopher Burrows/Alamy: p. 25 (right); David R. Frazier Photolibrary, Inc. / Alamy: p. 22; Garden World Images Ltd/Alamy: p. 25 (left); Holmes Garden Photos/Alamy: p. 24 (bottom); D. Hurst/Alamy: p. 27 (top); Richard Levine/Alamy: p. 17 (bottom), p. 26 (left); AP Photo/Luis M. Alvarez: p. 23 (bottom); AP Photo/Robert F. Bukaty: p. 18; AP Photo/Gary Kazanjian: p. 23 (top); AP Photo/Santiago Lyon: p. 5 (bottom); AP Photo/Statesman Journal, Thomas Patterson: p. 25 (top); Andy Warhol Foundation/ Corbis: p. 27 (bottom); Yann Arthus-Bertrand/Corbis: p. 7 (bottom); Bettmann/Corbis: p. 15 (top); Eric Crichton/Corbis: p. 21 (top);Gianni Dagli Orti/Corbis: p. 11; Ric Ergenbright/Corbis: p. 7 (top); Michelle Garrett/Corbis: p. 6; Richard Hamilton Smith/Corbis: cover; Wu Hong/epa/Corbis: p. 31 (bottom); Patrick Johns/Corbis: p. 9 (top); Richard T. Nowitz/Corbis: p. 14; Roman Soumar/Corbis: p. 10; Liba Taylor/Corbis: p. 9 (bottom); Getty Images/Michael Blann: p. 21; Getty Images/Photo by Hulton Archive: p. 17 (top); Getty Images/David Silverman: p. 30; The Granger Collection, New York: p. 12, p. 13, p. 15 (bottom); Adrianna Morganelli: p. 1, p. 3; Ohio Historical Society: p. 16; Martin Bond/Photo Researchers, Inc.: p. 31 (top); Nigel Cattlin/ Photo Researchers, Inc.: p. 19 (bottom), p. 28 (top), p. 29 (bottom); Maryann Frazier/Photo Researchers, Inc.: p. 19 (top); Michael P. Gadomski/Photo Researchers, Inc.: p. 24 (top); John Kaprielian/Photo Researchers, Inc.: p. 8 (top); Gregory Ochocki/Photo Researchers, Inc.: p. 29 (top); Other images from Stock CD.

Cartography: Jim Chernishenko: p. 6

Cover: Farmers harvesting tomatoes on a large tomato farm.

Title page: This woman is cutting up tomatoes to make homemade tomato sauce.

Contents page: Indeterminate, or tall-growing, tomato plants do not have strong stems and have to be supported while they grow.

Library and Archives Canada Cataloguing in Publication

Morganelli, Adrianna, 1979-
    The biography of tomatoes / Adrianna Morganelli.

(How did that get here?)
Includes index.
ISBN 978-0-7787-2494-0 (bound)
ISBN 978-0-7787-2530-5 (pbk.)

    1. Tomatoes--Juvenile literature. I. Title. II. Series.

SB349.M66 2007   j635'.642   C2007-901720-7

Library of Congress Cataloging-in-Publication Data

Morganelli, Adrianna, 1979-
    The biography of tomatoes / written by Adrianna Morganelli.
       p. cm. -- (How did that get here?)
    Includes index.
    ISBN-13: 978-0-7787-2494-0 (rlb)
    ISBN-10: 0-7787-2494-8 (rlb)
    ISBN-13: 978-0-7787-2530-5 (pb)
    ISBN-10: 0-7787-2530-8 (pb)
    1. Tomatoes. 2. Tomatoes--History. I. Title. II. Series.

SB349.M66 2007
635'.642--dc22   2007011219

Crabtree Publishing Company

www.crabtreebooks.com   1-800-387-7650

Published in Canada
Crabtree Publishing
616 Welland Ave.
St. Catharines, ON
L2M 5V6

Published in the United States
Crabtree Publishing
PMB16A
350 Fifth Ave., Suite 3308
New York, NY 10118

Published in the United Kingdom
Crabtree Publishing
White Cross Mills
High Town, Lancaster
LA1 4XS

Published in Australia
Crabtree Publishing
386 Mt. Alexander Rd.
Ascot Vale (Melbourne)
VIC 3032

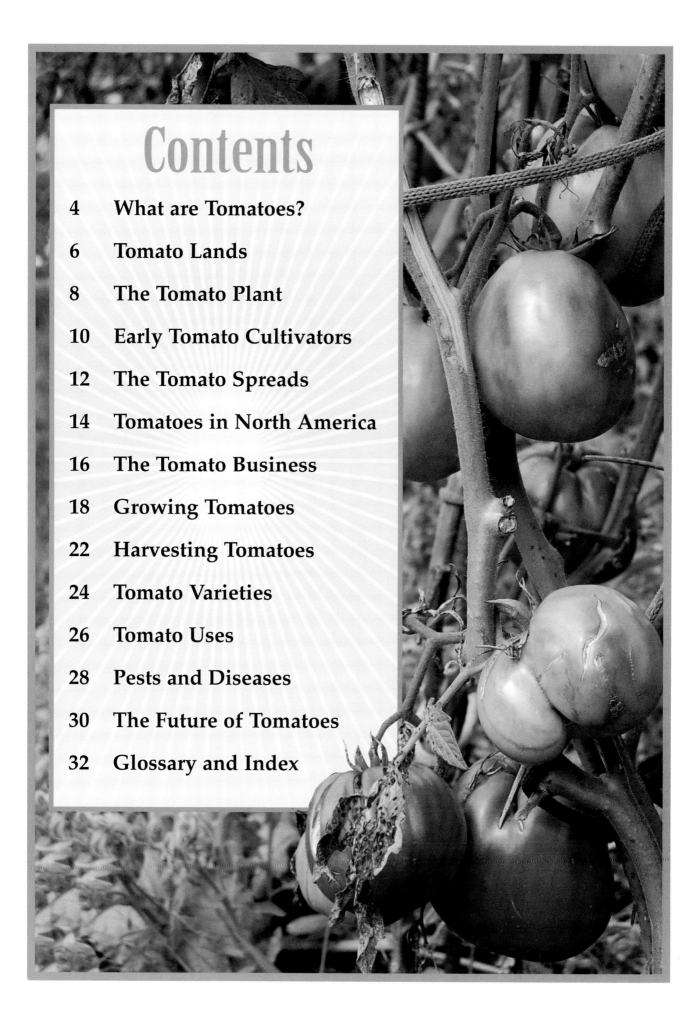

Contents

What are Tomatoes?

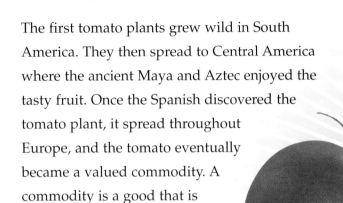

The first tomato plants grew wild in South America. They then spread to Central America where the ancient Maya and Aztec enjoyed the tasty fruit. Once the Spanish discovered the tomato plant, it spread throughout Europe, and the tomato eventually became a valued commodity. A commodity is a good that is bought and sold on world markets. Today, there is a high demand for tomatoes, and they are grown all over the world on **commercial** farms and in greenhouses. Many people around the world grow tomatoes in household gardens, where tomatoes are left to ripen on the vines. This gives the fruit a better flavor than commercially grown tomatoes, which are picked when they are green and unripe. Commercially grown tomatoes ripen while they are being shipped to **distributors** and grocery stores.

Tomatoes Around the World

Tomatoes are rich in minerals and vitamins, including vitamins A and C, and lose very little of their **nutrients** when they are cooked. Tomatoes are eaten all over the world, and are an important ingredient in Middle Eastern and Mediterranean cooking. In the Catalonia region of Spain, tomatoes are used to make *pa amb tomàquet*, which is bread that has been rubbed with tomatoes and seasoned with olive oil and salt. Tomato sauce is popular in Italy, where it is eaten over meat, vegetables, on pizza, and in pasta dishes. Tomatoes are also used to make juices, soups, ketchup, and **pastes**.

▲ *Flavorful vine-ripened tomatoes are grown in people's gardens around the world.*

◀ *Gazpacho is a cold soup made from tomatoes. The dish originated in Spain.*

Vegetable or Fruit?

The tomato is commonly referred to as a vegetable, but it is actually the fruit of a vine. Edible plants that carry seeds used for **reproduction**, such as watermelons, grapes, and tomatoes, are fruits. In 1893, the United States Supreme Court ruled that the tomato is a vegetable because it is eaten as part of a main course of a meal, rather than as a dessert as most other fruits are. At the time, all vegetables that were **imported** into the United States were **taxed**, but fruits were not. The Supreme Court's decision caused a decrease in the amount of tomatoes imported from Cuba and Mexico. Many American tomato growers grew very wealthy because they became the country's primary suppliers of tomatoes.

▲ *Other fruits that are referred to as vegetables include cucumbers, eggplant, and pumpkins.*

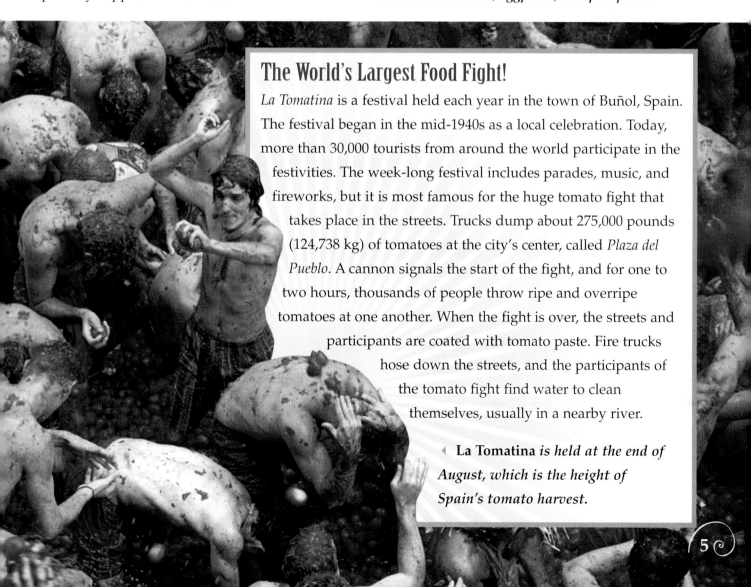

The World's Largest Food Fight!

La Tomatina is a festival held each year in the town of Buñol, Spain. The festival began in the mid-1940s as a local celebration. Today, more than 30,000 tourists from around the world participate in the festivities. The week-long festival includes parades, music, and fireworks, but it is most famous for the huge tomato fight that takes place in the streets. Trucks dump about 275,000 pounds (124,738 kg) of tomatoes at the city's center, called *Plaza del Pueblo*. A cannon signals the start of the fight, and for one to two hours, thousands of people throw ripe and overripe tomatoes at one another. When the fight is over, the streets and participants are coated with tomato paste. Fire trucks hose down the streets, and the participants of the tomato fight find water to clean themselves, usually in a nearby river.

◀ **La Tomatina** *is held at the end of August, which is the height of Spain's tomato harvest.*

Tomato Lands

Scientists believe that the tomato plant first grew wild in the Andes Mountains in Peru, in South America. Today, due to the high demand for tomatoes, the plant is grown in countries all over the world where the climate is warm. Tomato crops are grown on large farms and in greenhouses. They are also grown on smaller family-owned farms and in home gardens.

▶ *The tomato plants first grown in Peru looked very similar to the cherry tomato plant. Tomato plants have changed into different varieties over time.*

(below) This map shows the major tomato producing countries in the world today.

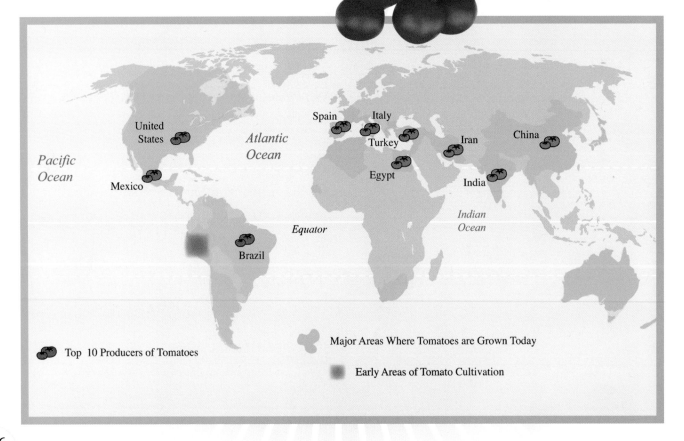

Top 10 Producers of Tomatoes

Major Areas Where Tomatoes are Grown Today

Early Areas of Tomato Cultivation

Top Growers

About 110 million tons (100 million tonnes) of tomatoes are cultivated worldwide each year. The tomato is the world's leading fruit for **processing** into food products. Tomatoes are made into sauces, juices, soups, and more. Most tomatoes are sold in markets to consumers. More than 25 percent of the world's tomatoes are processed to make food products. Many countries cultivate tomatoes, but the top producers are China, the United States, and Turkey. Italy, India, Egypt, and Spain also produce much of the world's tomatoes. In the United States, California is the top tomato-producing state. California uses more than 200 square miles (322 square km) of land to cultivate tomatoes, and produces more than 90 percent of the country's tomatoes.

Top Consumers

Many countries around the world import tomatoes from other countries. The United States is one of the top importers and exporters of tomatoes. This is because only some of the warmer southern states are able to grow tomatoes year-round, and many states are limited to growing crops only during warm summer months. Other main tomato importers include Germany, the United Kingdom, France, and the Netherlands.

▲ *A farm worker in China harvests tomatoes.*

(right) Farmers gather tomatoes from a farm in Egypt.

The Tomato Plant

The tomato plant's scientific name is *Solanum lycopersicon*. The plant produces blossoms, which are yellow in most varieties, or plant types. The tomato blossom is called a "perfect flower," because it has both male and female parts, and is able to produce pollen. Once the tomato blossom is **pollinated**, the petals die and fall off the plant, and a tomato begins to form in the blossom's center.

The Fruit

The edible part of the tomato plant is called the fruit. Different varieties of plants have fruits of varying sizes, shapes, and colors. The fruit is green when unripe and, in many varieties, ranges in color from yellow, orange, and red when ripe. When left to ripen on the vine, the sugars, **acids**, and oils inside the fruit work together to create the tomato's flavor. Tomatoes are rich in lycopene, which is a **pigment** that gives the skin a red color. Beneath the skin, there are two or more hollow compartments called locules. Locules are filled with a gelatin-like substance that surrounds the seeds.

(top) Most tomato plants produce yellow blossoms, or flowers.

◀ *Inside the tomato there are from two to ten locules, depending on the variety. This one has three.*

8

Tall-Growing Plants

There are two main types of tomato plants: indeterminate and determinate. Indeterminate plants, also called tall-growing plants, grow from six to ten feet (1.8 to three meters) high, and take up a lot of space in fields and gardens. They do not have strong stems, so many of the tomatoes rest on the ground, where they are vulnerable to rotting and being eaten by insects and other pests. To protect the fruit, growers use stakes, **trellises**, or wire cages to support the plant. They also prune, or cut back, the plant to two or three main stems. The many leaves of indeterminate plants protect the fruits from the hot Sun, which also means that the fruits ripen slowly. At any one time, an indeterminate tomato plant may have tomatoes at different stages of development. Growers continually pick tomatoes from the plant during a harvest period that lasts several months.

Determinate

Determinate tomato plants, also called bush tomatoes, are smaller than indeterminate plants. They grow to about three feet (0.9 meters) high. The fruits ripen quickly because the plants have fewer leaves and the fruits are exposed to the Sun. All of the fruit develops at around the same time, so growers can harvest all their crop during a short time, from about two to three weeks.

(top) Bush tomatoes are popular with commercial growers because their small size takes up little room on farms. This allows growers to plant more crops and yield, or produce, more tomatoes.

(left) A worker ties a young indeterminate tomato plant to a wooden stake for support.

Early Tomato Cultivators

Historians believe that the tomato plant originated in South America, in the areas surrounding the Andes Mountains, which includes parts of Peru, Ecuador, Bolivia, Chile, and Colombia. Early tomatoes were similar to cherry tomatoes today. The fruits of the plant grew in clusters, and were red and very small. It is believed that early Andean **civilizations** did not cultivate the tomato or use it as a food source. Early civilizations commonly decorated pottery and **textiles** with descriptions and images of important crops and figures, but none that have been found depict the tomato plant. In addition, there is no word in early South American languages for the tomato.

The Maya

The tomato plant spread to Mexico. Some scientists believe the plant spread by birds and animals carrying the seeds of the plant. The Maya, an ancient civilization that lived in southern Mexico between 250 A.D. and 950 A.D., were the first to cultivate the tomato plant. They called it *tomatl* or *xtomatl*. The Maya selected and planted the seeds of the best tomatoes to create tomato plants that had larger and tastier fruits. The Maya commonly used *milpa* farming to grow their crops. *Milpa* farming involves clearing forests and burning the vegetation. The ash of the burned plants **fertilized** the soil by returning nutrients to it.

By the 1500s, new varieties of tomatoes were reintroduced to the Andes. The plants were grown on terraces, which were plots of land that looked like steps cut into the mountainsides.

Maya Farming Villages

Joya de Cerén, in El Salvador, is the site of an ancient Maya farming village where tomatoes and other crops were cultivated. **Archaeologists** have uncovered the remains of food, utensils, and ceramics at Joya de Cerén. These items were preserved under the ash of the Lona Caldera volcano, which erupted around 600 A.D. By studying the remains, archaeologists have concluded that many Maya cultivated the tomato plant, as well as chili peppers and herbs, in small household gardens.

The Aztec used simple tools, such as wooden hoes and sticks for digging, to tend their food crops on the **chinampas.**

The Aztec

The Maya traded the seeds of tomato plants that had yellow fruits to the Aztec. The Aztec lived in central Mexico from 1200 to the early 1500s. These tomatoes looked similar to another fruit the Aztec ate, called the husk tomato, or the "tomatillo." The Aztec made salsa with the tomato by extracting the juice from the fruit, and mixing the flesh with chili peppers and ground pumpkin seeds. The Aztec grew tomato crops on farms called *chinampas* in their capital city, Tenochtitlan, which was built on an island in Lake Texcoco. They placed frames of woven reeds on top of the water, and piled soil on top. Trees were planted around the frames, and their roots secured the soil and kept the soil from washing away. In addition to planting tomatoes, the Aztec planted squash, potatoes, and corn.

The Tomato Spreads

The period of time between the 1400s and the 1600s is known as the Age of Exploration. During this time, European explorers set sail in search of new lands to claim for their countries, new trade routes, and valuable goods. In 1519, Spanish **conquistador** Hernando Cortés arrived in the Aztec capital city of Tenochtitlan, which is now Mexico City, where he discovered the tomato plant. The fruit of the tomato plant that the Aztec were cultivating were large and yellow. When Cortés returned to Spain, he presented the king with tomato seeds.

First Impressions

When the tomato plant was introduced to Spain, people were afraid to eat the fruit. They believed the tomato was toxic, or poisonous. The tomato, which the Spanish called *tomate*, was used for decoration, and not for eating. The plants were grown in pots and displayed in people's homes, and were used to decorate outhouses and **arbors**.

▼ *When Europeans met the Native peoples in the New World, they were introduced to a great variety of new plants and animals.*

(above) During the 1500s, tomatoes were sometimes used in Europe to cure ailments. The juice extracted from the stems and leaves of the plant were used to treat skin diseases.

Southern Europe

Through trade, the tomato spread to other countries in southern Europe, including Italy, Turkey, Portugal, and Greece. The tomato plant grew well in the warm climate. Many European physicians warned that the tomato provided little nourishment if eaten, and caused many ailments, including **apoplexy**, fainting, and stomachaches. Despite these warnings, historians believe that the Italians were the first Europeans to use tomatoes in their cooking. Italians called the tomato *pomodoro*, which means "golden apple." Eventually, people throughout southern Europe began incorporating tomatoes into their cooking, including using them to make sauces, and frying them in oil and seasoning them with salt and pepper.

Northern Europe

Tomatoes were not eaten in northern Europe until the 1700s. People first grew tomato plants to decorate their homes and other structures, as southern Europeans had. People were suspicious of tomatoes because they did not look like other fruits and vegetables they grew. Tomatoes were also not recommended for consumption by many physicians. They believed that tomatoes should not be eaten in northern Europe because they were a "cool" fruit, better suited to people living in the warmer climates of southern Europe. When northern Europeans visited southern Europe, they ate tomatoes, and brought back a taste for the fruit when they returned home. By the mid-1700s, the tomato was cultivated in northern Europe as a food crop.

Tomatoes in North America

Europeans introduced the tomato plant to their **colonies** in North, Central, and South America. In what is now the southern United States, European colonists began cultivating the plant as a food crop. By the late 1700s, recipes featuring the tomato as an ingredient appeared in cookbooks, and some farm markets also offered tomatoes for sale. In the north, people did not adopt the tomato as a food right away. They were suspicious of the fruit because it was unlike other fruits they were eating. The tomato plant did not grow well in the climate, and the fruit took a long time to mature.

(above) In the 1780s, American president Thomas Jefferson grew tomato plants in his gardens at his estate, Monticello, in Virginia.

Tomato Craze

In 1834, an American doctor named John Cook Bennett declared that the tomato could cure many ailments, including **dyspepsia** and **cholera**. His theories were published in medical journals and newspapers in the United States. Bennett met Alexander Miles, who was selling a pill called the "American Hygiene Pill." Bennett suggested that Miles rename his medicine "Extract of Tomato." Miles advertised his pill as having the ability to cure many ailments and diseases. This created a tomato craze in the United States. In the 1840s, an investigation into the pill found that it contained no trace of tomatoes. Despite these findings, people throughout North America began to accept the tomato as a delicious and wholesome food.

European Influence

The popularity of the tomato increased when **immigrants** arrived in North America from Europe. The European immigrants, many from Italy and France, were accustomed to eating tomatoes in their countries, and helped introduce a taste for the fruit throughout the United States. They grew tomato plants in home gardens, and purchased them at markets. The European immigrants ate the fruit plain, and used them to make **preserves** and sauces.

(right) Italian immigrants arriving in New York in 1920. The cuisine that they brought with them included using tomatoes, which helped make tomatoes popular in North America.

Squashing the Myth

According to legend, a man named Robert Gibbon Johnson from Salem, New Jersey, helped disprove the myth that the tomato was poisonous and fatal if eaten. The townspeople of Salem believed that eating the tomato would result in death. In 1820, Johnson ate a basket of tomatoes from his garden on the steps of the local courthouse in front of the townspeople. When the townspeople saw that Johnson survived after eating the fruit, people began to accept the tomato as a food.

▶ *The tomato plant is a member of the Solanaceae, or nightshade plant, family. Some of the other plants in this family include potatoes, peppers, and eggplant.*

Throughout the 1800s, the tomato grew in popularity in North America. Seed companies, which produce and sell seeds, began to create new varieties of the tomato plant in the 1860s to be grown as commercial crops. Many early tomato plants bore small, misshapen fruit that had little flavor. Seed companies created new varieties of tomato plants using **cross-pollination**. By 1900, seed companies had created new plants with large, smooth fruit that had a balance of sweetness and acidity. The seeds were sold to farmers across North America, who grew tomato crops on large farms.

Canneries

By the mid-1800s, canneries were established throughout North America. A cannery is a factory where foods are sealed in airtight cans and heated to prevent the food inside from spoiling. Many food products began to be mass produced, including peeled canned tomatoes. Canning tomatoes allowed people to enjoy the fruit year-round. One of the most successful canned tomato products was soup. In 1897, a scientist named John T. Dorrance began working for the Campbell Soup Company, which produced canned tomatoes, soups, and minced meats. Dorrance created a process for condensing soup, which involved removing half of the water from the soup to create a thicker consistency. During the first year of production, the company sold five soup flavors, including tomato, chicken, vegetable, consommé, and oxtail. By 1904, they were offering over 20 different flavors, and were selling about 16 million cans of soup a year.

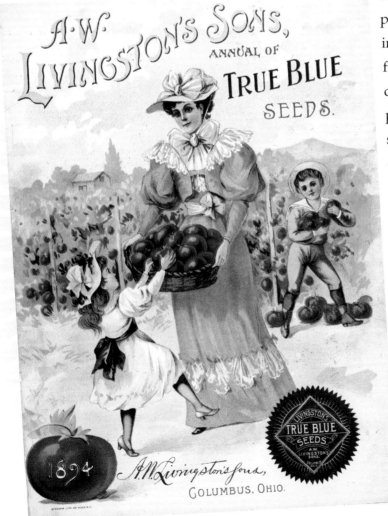

◄ *Alexander W. Livingston from Reynoldsburg, Ohio, created more than 30 varieties of tomato plants. In 1870, Livingston introduced his first variety, called the Paragon. The Paragon is known as the first perfectly smooth, deep red tomato grown in North America.*

During the Great Depression, a time of severe economic hardship in the 1930s, tomato soup was the top food item consumed. Each can of soup cost only 12 cents and provided a healthy meal.

Growth of Commercial Tomatoes

By the 1940s, the tomato business in North America was flourishing. Farmers cultivated tomato crops and sold their produce to grocers and companies that processed them into food products. The consumer demand for tomatoes was high. Seed companies created new varieties of tomato plants that produced all their fruit at the same time, allowing farmers to harvest their crops in a shorter amount of time and keep labor costs down. Farmers harvested their crops before the fruit were fully ripe. Ripe tomatoes are more fragile and can spoil before reaching their destination. Not allowing tomatoes to ripen on the vines made them less flavorful. New plant varieties also produced firmer fruit that did not bruise as easily during harvest and shipping. Preventing tomatoes from being mashed and split was important for displaying tomatoes for sale. Many of these advancements also made the new tomato varieties less tasty.

Heinz Tomato Ketchup

Tomatoes are used to make condiments, such as ketchup. Condiments are added to food to enhance or improve flavor. In North America, companies began manufacturing tomato ketchups by the 1830s. In 1876, the H.J. Heinz Company in Pennsylvania launched their tomato ketchup. Heinz ketchup was thicker and had more of a vinegary taste than early commercial ketchups, and became popular with consumers. Today, 650 million bottles of Heinz tomato ketchup are sold worldwide each year.

17

Growing Tomatoes

In tomato growing countries that have cold winters, the plants are grown as annuals. Annuals are plants that survive for only one growing season. In many countries that experience cool seasons, the plants are killed by frost in late fall. The plants grow best in temperatures ranging from 55° to 75° Fahrenheit (13° to 24° Celsius) and need six or seven hours of sunlight a day. When tomato plants are exposed to lower temperatures, they develop less flavorful fruit. Plants that are exposed to high temperatures develop uneven color or can rot. Tomatoes need a continuous supply of water, and loose, **fertile** soil to grow in.

Greenhouses

Tomatoes are often grown in greenhouses in areas with cooler climates. Greenhouses are rooms or buildings made of glass or plastic that retain the heat from the Sun to create a warm growing environment. Tomato seeds are planted in individual containers filled with soil. After about one week, the seeds begin to germinate, or sprout seedlings. The seedlings grow for about four to six weeks, at which time they are large enough to be transplanted in soil-filled rows inside the greenhouse. **Irrigation** systems are used to provide water and nutrients to the plants.

Many people buy greenhouse-grown tomatoes. In greenhouses, the fruits are left to ripen on the vine until they are picked, and are sold directly to markets. Allowing tomatoes to ripen on the vine greatly improves the flavor of the fruit.

Greenhouse Pollination

Fans are used to circulate, or move around, the air in greenhouses. Moving air helps pollinate the plants. The pollen is light enough to be carried by the air to the part of the flower that receives the pollen. Some greenhouses also practice mechanical pollination. In mechanical pollination, greenhouse workers use hand-held machines to pollinate each plant. Tomato flowers open at different times, which requires workers to continually check if they are ready to be pollinated. Since the mid-1990s, bumblebees have been used for pollination in North American greenhouses. Bumblebees are usually more efficient at pollinating all of the flowers on a plant. This results in higher tomato yields than are achieved with mechanical pollination.

▲ *Bumblebees pollinate up to 30 tomato flowers a minute.*

Hydroponic Farming

Many greenhouses grow tomato plants using hydroponic farming. Instead of growing plants in soil, hydroponic tomato plants are grown in a solution of water and nutrients. In soil-grown crops, the soil contains nutrients that are absorbed by the plants' roots. When nutrients are added to a hydroponic plant's water supply, soil is not needed. Hydroponic farming eliminates weeds, the need for irrigation systems, and requires less **pesticides**. Hydroponic tomatoes can either be grown by suspending the plant's roots in water, or by using rocks or pebbles to support the roots.

(right) These hydroponic tomato plants are being grown in a greenhouse. The plants' roots are supported by rockwool, which is a type of rock. The pipes supply the plants with nutrient-rich water.

Commercial Farms

Most commercial tomato crops are grown on large farms. The tomato seeds are planted in greenhouses in small containers or trays to germinate. Once the seedlings grow to about 1.5 inches (3.8 cm) tall, they are transplanted to new containers, where they are left to grow for about seven to eight weeks. Tomato plants are then planted in fields about 14 inches (36 centimeters) apart in rows. As the plants grow, the leaves provide shade for one another, which keeps the roots cool, and reduces overexposure to the Sun. Field tomato plants require about one inch (three centimeters) of water a week, provided by rainfall or irrigation systems. They are pruned regularly, and are supported by wooden or metal stakes.

(background) A tomato farm's irrigation system.

Organic Farming

Many commercial farmers spray chemicals on their crops, such as pesticides and insecticides to ward off harmful insects, and herbicides to destroy weeds. These chemicals can pollute soil and nearby water sources. Today, more farmers are growing tomato crops organically, which includes methods that are less harmful to the environment. Organic fertilizers such as animal manure and dead leaves are used to supply the soil with nutrients. Organic farmers also rotate their crops from year to year, or plant them in different fields. Crop rotation helps prevent the soil from being depleted of its nutrients.

Home Gardens

Many people worldwide grow tomato plants in home gardens. Homegrown tomatoes usually taste better than commercial tomatoes since they are left to ripen on the vine until they are ready to be eaten. There are a number of tomato plant varieties available to home gardeners. Gardeners are able to choose varieties that will grow best in the areas they live in.

(above) A home garden with tomato plants supported by tall stakes.

(left) Organically-grown tomatoes look the same as other tomatoes. The difference is that these tomatoes are grown using more environmentally-friendly practices.

Harvesting Tomatoes

Tomatoes grown on commercial farms for processing are left to ripen on the vine. The tomatoes are harvested by machines that travel between the rows of tomato plants in the field. The machines cut down the whole tomato plant, shake the tomatoes off the vine, and transfer them to a bin. Tomatoes grown for sale in fresh food markets are handpicked when they are green and unripe. Workers remove the fruits from the plants by gently twisting them off the vine without tearing or damaging the fruits.

Sorting, Grading, and Washing

Tomatoes that are sent to factories for processing are sorted and graded by shape, color, and size. Workers inspect the tomatoes for defects. Tomatoes that are rotten, damaged, or misshapen are removed. In some countries, tomatoes are sorted and graded by hand. In other countries, these jobs are performed by machines. The tomatoes are then thoroughly washed to remove any dirt from the fields. The tomatoes are sprayed with **chlorinated** water as they move along a conveyor belt.

(above) Tomatoes that will be sold directly to a factory to be processed into sauces and soups are loaded into a bin during harvest.

Gassing with Ethylene

Unripe tomatoes are kept in rooms that are pumped with ethylene to speed ripening. Ethylene is a ripening agent that many fruits produce naturally. Tomatoes that are artificially ripened with ethylene keep longer, but they usually have a poorer flavor and starchier texture than tomatoes that have ripened on the vine. The tomatoes are exposed to ethylene for one to two days until their skins develop a faint pink color. They are then loaded onto trucks to be shipped to consumers. The ripening process continues during shipping.

▲ *Each truck holds about 50,000 pounds (22,680 kilograms) of tomatoes.*

Tomato Workers

Tomato farms are large commercial operations, and require many workers, especially on farms where tomatoes are cultivated by hand. Growing and harvesting tomatoes is a billion dollar industry, but laborers who work on tomato farms receive little money for their labor. On some farms where tomatoes are grown, such as in Canada and the United States, workers from other countries are brought in to harvest the crops. These workers are known as migrant farm workers. They often come from poorer countries such as Mexico or Jamaica.

◀ *A farm worker carries a bushel of tomatoes that have just been picked.*

Tomato Varieties

There are more than 5,000 different varieties of tomato plants. In the Andes Mountains, where the tomato plant originated, new tomato varieties were created through the process of natural cross-pollination. Sometimes, the **genetic codes** of the plants became altered and new plant varieties were produced.

Early Cultivators

The ancient civilizations that first cultivated the tomato plant used a process called selection, or selective breeding, to create new varieties of tomato plants. The seeds of the healthiest tomato plants in a crop were used to plant new crops. Once Europeans introduced the tomato plant to other parts of the world, selective breeding was also used to create plants that had desirable characteristics. The seeds of tomato plants that had favorable qualities, such as large fruits or a resistance to a disease, were selected and replanted. Through many years of selection, many undesirable qualities were bred out and new plant varieties were developed.

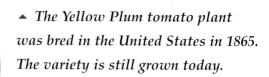

▲ The Yellow Plum tomato plant was bred in the United States in 1865. The variety is still grown today.

◄ The many varieties of tomato plants produce fruits of various colors. The skin and flesh of the Great White tomato variety is creamy white when ripe.

Tomato Hybrids

In the 1940s, many seed companies in North America used cross-pollination to create new tomato plant varieties. In cross-pollination, the pollen from one variety of tomato plant is used to pollinate another tomato plant variety. The seed that is produced grows into a new plant, called a hybrid plant, which has the characteristics of both parent plants. Hybrid tomato plants are bred to create fruit of various sizes, shapes, colors, and flavors. Many varieties are also resistant to specific diseases, can grow in different types of environments, or are bred to suit the needs of food processing companies.

(right) A new variety of the tomato plant with purple fruit has been created.

Heirloom Tomatoes

Heirloom tomatoes are varieties of tomato plants that have been open-pollinated. This means that the pollination is achieved naturally by insects, animals, or the wind. Hundreds of heirloom tomatoes are still available today, but most have become extinct because they have been altered through breeding. Many organizations around the world work to protect and preserve the remaining varieties of heirloom tomatoes still in existence. Some heirloom tomatoes include the Hawaiian Pineapple, the Black Krim, and the Big Beef.

(left) An heirloom tomato variety called Purple Calabash.

▸ *The long, green and yellow fruit of the Green Sausage heirloom variety.*

Tomato Uses

Tomatoes are used to create many delicious dishes in countries around the world. Many people eat tomatoes raw, or add them to omelets, salads, and stews. Tomatoes are also consumed for their health benefits. Tomatoes contain an **antioxidant** called lycopene, which has been found to help protect people from a deadly disease called cancer.

Ketchup

Ketchup is a thick paste made of ripened tomatoes. Other ingredients added to most ketchups include vinegar, salt, sugar, cloves, and cinnamon. In North America, ketchup is commonly used as a condiment to add flavor to foods such as hamburgers and fries. Ketchup is often used as a main ingredient for barbecue sauces, especially in the southern United States.

(below) Tomato sauces are used to make pizza. The first pizza parlors, or pizzerias, opened in New York City in the early 1900s.

Tomato Sauce

Tomato sauces are made of chopped tomatoes that have had their skins and seeds removed. The Plum tomato is a common variety used to make sauces, because it has few seeds and a dense flesh. Tomato sauces are cooked with onions and garlic, and are seasoned with herbs such as basil, oregano, and parsley. The sauces are poured over pastas, spread on pizzas, and eaten with meat and vegetables. Italian cooking features many types of tomato sauces, including Bolognese sauce, which also contains ground meat.

▲ *Ketchup is a popular condiment for hot dogs.*

▼ *Many pasta dishes include tomatoes.*

Tomato Juice

The juice of squeezed tomatoes is served as a beverage. It is drunk plain, or mixed with alcohol to make adult drinks. Many tomato juice manufacturers add salt to their juices for added flavor. Other ingredients usually added to tomato juice include garlic powder and onion powder. In addition to drinking tomato juice for its flavor, many people also drink the juice because it is rich in lycopene. Tomato juice is also added to canned tomatoes.

▸ *Tomato juice is a healthy beverage.*

Tomato Purée

Tomato purée is a smooth, creamy paste usually made only with tomatoes. To make tomato purée, tomatoes are washed and their stems and leaves removed. The tomatoes are then chopped and mashed to a desired consistency. Tomato purée is used to flavor stews, sauces, and soups.

Tomato Soup

Tomato soup is a soup made from chunks of tomato or tomato purée. Tomato soup is commonly served hot, but some tomato soups are eaten cold, such as gazpacho soup. Canned condensed tomato soups are popular, especially in North America. Many toppings are served with tomato soup, including crackers, sour cream, and cheese.

◂ *Campbell's is one of the most popular soup brands in North America.*

Pests and Diseases

Growing healthy tomato crops can be challenging. Tomato crops are constantly threatened by disease, insect infestation, and unfavorable weather conditions. The greatest threat to the health of tomato plants are diseases caused by bacteria, fungi, and viruses. Growers can minimize disease by planting varieties that have an increased resistance to some diseases, but no variety is resistant to all diseases. Removing infected plants from gardens, greenhouses, and farms can reduce the spread of disease to healthy plants.

(right) Tomato late blight is a plant disease that can kill entire tomato crops. The disease causes dark spots to form on the stems, leaves, and fruit, and mold to grow on the underside of the leaves.

▼ Backyard animals such as raccoons, squirrels, and moles, eat ripe tomatoes from the vine.

Common Diseases

Two common tomato plant diseases caused by fungi are verticillium wilt and fusarium wilt. Plants suffering from verticillium wilt can still produce tomatoes, but the fruit produced are small. The leaves of the plant turn yellow, wilt, and eventually fall off. The loss of leaves exposes the fruit to too much Sun, which leaves them at risk for sunscald. Fusarium wilt is a much more serious disease that can wipe out an entire tomato crop. It is a fungus found in the soil that tomato plants grow in. The disease can affect plants at all stages of development. Early symptoms include yellowing of the lower leaves, which eventually wilt and die. As the disease progresses, the fungus travels up the plant, destroying it until it dies.

Insects

Many types of insects damage tomato plants. Common pests of the tomato plant include whiteflies, which suck the sap from the leaves, and excrete a sticky substance called honeydew on the leaves and fruit. A black fungus grows on the honeydew, which harms the tomato plant. Nematodes are tiny worms that feed on the roots of tomato plants, causing the plants to wilt and their growth to be stunted. Harmful insects can be controlled using pesticides and by removing the weeds that insects commonly breed and live in. Some other types of plants are grown near tomato plants to help repel pests. For example, marigold plants ward off nematodes from the surrounding soil. Some insects are beneficial to plants by feeding on harmful insects. These insects are introduced to greenhouses, farms, and home gardens.

(above) The tomato hornworm is the larva of a moth that damages tomato plants by feeding on the fruits and leaves.

Other Tomato Troubles

Temperature and the amount of rainfall and nutrients in the soil, determine whether a tomato crop will be healthy. Sunscald is the yellowing of the fruit's skin due to overexposure to the Sun. With too much water, tomatoes can develop blossom end rot. Tomatoes with blossom end rot have dark and sunken areas on the bottom of the fruit. Blossom drop is a condition in which the blossoms of the plant drop off before tomatoes start to grow. This is caused by extreme temperatures or water levels. If young tomato plants are exposed to cold temperatures, the fruit may have dark green or brown scars, indents, and swollen bulges. Tomato plants exposed to temperatures below 40° Fahrenheit (4° Celsius) will die.

(right) A tomato plant with blossom end rot.

The Future of Tomatoes

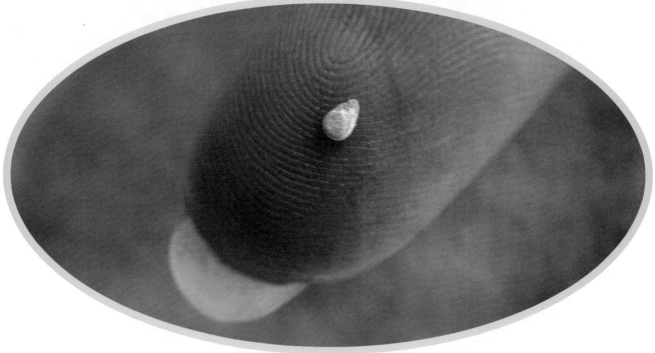

Scientists have discovered particular **genes** in tomatoes that are responsible for different characteristics. Scientists create new types of tomato plants by changing, or modifying, the plants' genes. These plants are called genetically modified organisms, or GMOs. The new tomato plants are created to have more beneficial traits, such as resistance to specific diseases and insects, and to last longer before spoiling. Some GMO tomato plants even have extra vitamins.

Flavr Savr

Tomatoes were the first genetically modified food sold in stores. The GMO tomato, called Flavr Savr, was introduced in 1994 in the United States, Canada, and Britain. Flavr Savr was bred to resist rotting, and to remain firm after harvest so that it could be left to ripen on the vine longer. Only three years later, the tomatoes were pulled off the market because they were too fragile and difficult to transport. Today, scientists are working to discover a way to modify tomato plants that are resistant to verticillium wilt and fusarium wilt, two of the most common diseases that plague tomato crops.

(above) Today, scientists make hybrid tomato plants to control fruit size and firmness, the amount of leaves on a plant, and disease resistance. This tiny seed is a hybrid tomato plant seed called Summer Sun. It was developed to have a sweeter taste than other types of tomatoes.

Future Hydroponics

Hydroponics was invented in the 1930s, but it is still a new technology. The future of hydroponics to grow tomato plants depends on many things. The systems used to produce the crops are currently more expensive than those used to produce field-grown crops. For more farmers to use hydroponic farming, improvements in technology, such as artificial lighting, are necessary, and equipment costs need to lower. Tomato yields can be increased if new plant varieties grown hydroponically are developed to better resist diseases and pests.

▲ *This greenhouse is heated using an environmentally-friendly energy source called* geothermal energy.

Space Tomatoes

Hydroponic farming is useful for growing food crops in harsh environments, including barren deserts, Arctic communities, and even outer space! Scientists at the National Aeronautics and Space Administration (NASA), in the United States, are conducting experiments to find the best way to grow food in space using hydroponics. The tomato-growing tests are being done to see if astronauts in space can grow their own food.

These "space tomatoes" were grown from seeds that were left in space on a satellite for six years. Researchers wanted to test the effects of space on the seeds.

Glossary

acid A chemical compound that has a sour taste

antioxidant A substance in food that helps prevent cell damage in humans

apoplexy A stroke, or the eruption of a blood vessel in the brain that cuts off the brain's oxygen supply

arbor A shaded place enclosed by a frame on which climbing plants grow

archaeologist A person who studies ancient cultures

cholera A contagious disease that causes vomiting, cramps, and diarrhea

chlorine A chemical used to purify water

civilization The way of life of a group of people in history

colony Land ruled by a distant country

commercial For a profit

conquistador A Spanish explorer from the 1500s

cross-pollination Using pollen from one plant to pollinate another plant

distributor A company that sells products or goods to a retailer, or store

dyspepsia The inability to digest food

fertile Able to produce abundant crops

fertilize To add nutrients to the soil to help plants grow

gene Part of an animal or plant cell that determines a characteristic that will be passed on to its offspring

genetic code The instructions in cells that define the organism's characteristics, or traits

geothermal energy A renewable energy created using steam heated deep under the Earth

immigrant A person who moves to another country

import To buy in from another country

irrigation A system for watering crops

New World The name given to North, Central, and South America by Europeans

nutrients Substances that help living things grow

paste A thick paste made from ripe tomatoes

pesticide A chemical used to kill harmful insects

pigment A substance that creates a specific color

pollinate Pollination is the process whereby seeds are created that can be planted to grow new tomato plants

preserves Fruit cooked with sugar to protect against spoiling

processed A good that is manufactured, or changed from its original state

reproduction Producing the next generation

tax Money collected from people by a government

textile Cloth

trellis A frame of crossed slats used to support or train plants

Index

Printed in the U.S.A.